THE CHINESE BOOK
OF ETIQUETTE AND CONDUCT
FOR WOMEN AND GIRLS ENTITLED

Instruction for Chinese Women and Girls

By
LADY TSAO

Translated from the Chinese by
MRS. S. L. BALDWIN

NEW YORK: . EATON & MAINS
CINCINNATI: . JENNINGS & PYE

CONTENTS

ILLUSTRATIONS

PREFACE

❧

FEW people in the West have any intelligent conception of the remarkable civilization that has existed in China for hundreds of years, and this in strange contrast with her squalor, poverty, and heathenism.

How little is known, save by a very few, of her reverence for parents, age, letters, and law ; of her teachers, schools, colleges, literary chancellors and degrees ; and that it is true in that great empire that the humblest may rise to be second only to the emperor if he has the ability. A literary aristocracy leads all others ; indeed, leaves no place for any other, and it is far more to have a literary degree than to be a millionaire. "Twice six hundred years has China's famed Hanlin Academy existed and been the Mecca of her aspiring scholars." Of what other countries can we find reliable dynastic histories of thousands of years, books on morals and etiquette, visiting cards, envelopes, tinted and decorated note paper, the very tint of the paper conveying sentiments of regard, and these not modern luxuries, but ancient, and in common use when our ancestors were such gross barbarians as no record proves the Chinese to have ever been? The better I know this wonderful people, and the more I study their history, the greater my astonishment that such a civilization can exist parallel with such degradation and superstition of the masses.

This is doubtless due to the exceptionally wise and good men they have had as teachers, notably Confucius and Mencius, whose instructions concerning all the relations of man to man are known and quoted from the highest down to the poorest classes.

I soon discovered that in our great

city of Foochow, in southern China, there was actually a circulating library. I think it is safe to say that such an institution could not be duplicated in any other heathen nation. I made haste through my native teacher to rent one of its most famous novels, in twelve booklets. I planned to translate it, with intent thus to become more familiar with the life and thought of the people and to compare their standards of life with our own. I was most interested to find the plan of the story very similar to those of our own writers. There were the same ideals for hero and heroine: lofty virtue, unfailing heroism, patient suffering, and self-sacrifice for "dear love's sake," on one side; and the most wicked selfishness, cunning, and scheming in the ever-present marplot. The hero was of high literary connections, himself distinguished for learning, honor, and bravery, the very idol and hope of his family. The heroine was a beautiful, refined young girl, also of literary family whom dire fortune had brought very low; and she as a last resort was ready to prove her filial affection—the central virtue of the Chinese—by consenting to be sold as a slave to save her father from imprisonment for debt by the vile man who wanted her. She abhorred this man, but seeing no other way to save her father was willing to sacrifice herself. The whole story was skillfully planned, beautifully worded, and intensely interesting. But alas! I never found time to complete the translation, and my last effort left my beautiful heroine in a perfect tangle of wicked schemes, while her deliverer, the hero, was at the bottom of a river in the care of a good goddess! I was comforted, however, by the assurance of my native teacher that our hero came up all right, and just at the very critical moment, demolished all the schemes of the wicked one, delivered the lovely heroine and her aged father, and, best of all, this story of the Orient ended in the same entrancing manner as those of the West, with marriage bells—nay, firecrackers innumerable and joy all around!

While forced to give up the completion of this famous Chinese work, the very name of which has slipped my memory, I did complete with even greater interest the translation of a far more famous work, the standard and universally prized book of *Instructions for Women and Girls*, said to be the first book of etiquette ever published, in which we find that this great people do not at all meet the popular conception of utterly degraded heathen. They have local books of etiquette printed in different dialects, of which there are about forty, but this standard work is in the classical or *book* language, and outranks all others, as well it may, for it includes far more than even the Western books of etiquette in its careful moral code.

China is certainly in advance of every other heathen nation, in that her wise men and women have ever lifted up a pure and good standard of life before the people. Confucius gave them the second table of the law—man's duty to man; but alas! knowing not the first—man's duty to God, and living many years before the revelation of Christ the Saviour, Exemplar, and Helper, neither Confucius nor his people could measure up to their own lofty standards.

I was often amused at my native assistant in the translation of this book. He had much national pride, great admiration for their ancient literary characters, and the most profound respect for the author of this book and her instructions. He was a first degree literary man, and withal an earnest and intelligent Christian, and manifested more satisfaction with Western ideas than any native I knew, but woman's seclusion, duty to obey, etc., he thoroughly approved, and regarded us Westerners as entirely too lax in these respects. So as the translation proceeded he would throw in remarks expressing his satisfaction at this or that, and at times even showing how *this* agreed with the Scriptures. Thus when it speaks of woman's duty to obey her husband and "listen with reverence to his words," he remarked with emphasis, "Just as Póló [Paul] taught, you see." I smiled and said nothing, but waited my opportunity to show him how far short they all came either of Paul's or his admired author's teachings, and the good chance came when the "instructions" spoke of husband and wife "sharing either riches or poverty." I said: "All this is very good in theory, but I do not see that your people practice it. So far from sharing poverty, you know how it is. If there are not enough vegetables and rice for all the family, the wife serves the husband with all he wants, then gives to the children, and too often all that is left for her is the water in which the vegetables were cooked. Paul says, 'The strong should bear the burdens of the weak.' Women are weak. Your author says, 'share poverty,' but I do not see that your people follow either the teaching of the one or the instructions of the other." He acknowledged the truth of this and that "there was still something lacking," but ever remained immovable in his conservatism on the " woman question."

In this translation the Chinese idiom has been retained as far as consistent with clearness of meaning.

The binding of the book is in conformity to Chinese thought. Bright scarlet is their joyful color—worn by the bride—the color of their visiting cards, and conspicuous in their wall decorations in temples and homes, and on all joyful occasions. The beautiful bamboo, which decorates the cover of the book and outlines the leaves, is also specially prized, and symbolizes peace ; the birds in the bamboo, messengers ; and we thus have the thought, messengers of peace, in harmony with the teaching of the book. Each illustration represents an important custom referred to in the chapter. These pictures and the design upon the cover were all made by a skilled Chinese artist, Mr. Pang Sun Yow, who has for years been a faithful member of one of the churches of Brooklyn.

BRIEF SKETCH OF THE AUTHORESS

PANG TAI KU was a very celebrated literary woman who lived in the Han dynasty about eighteen hundred and twenty years ago. Her father was a high official at the capital, then the city of Si-ngan, in the province of Shen-si. Pang Tai Ku was betrothed to a man of the Tsao family named Sin. Tsao Sin attained the highest literary degree, but, alas! died early, leaving Pang Tai Ku a lonely widow. Her elder brother, Pang Ku, was the president of the great Hanlin College, the first college of the empire and the only college to give the highest degree. He had commenced writing the history of the Han dynasty, but before he had completed the half he became totally blind. The emperor asked him who could complete the work. Pang Ku replied, "Under the whole heavens there is but one person who can do it—my younger sister, Tsao Tai Ku" (her name after marriage). At this time she was still in seclusion and mourning for her husband, although several years had passed since his death. The emperor sent her many valuable presents, invited her to come to the court, and built her a palace within the imperial grounds, but so humble was she that she attributed all of these honors to the emperor's regard for her brother, Pang Ku. She completed the history of the Han dynasty, and did it so well that no one could tell where her brother stopped and she began. The emperor was greatly pleased with her work and treated her with the highest respect and honor. He commanded all the ladies of the palace to do her reverence and to call her "Instructor of Women." He also requested her to teach these ladies.

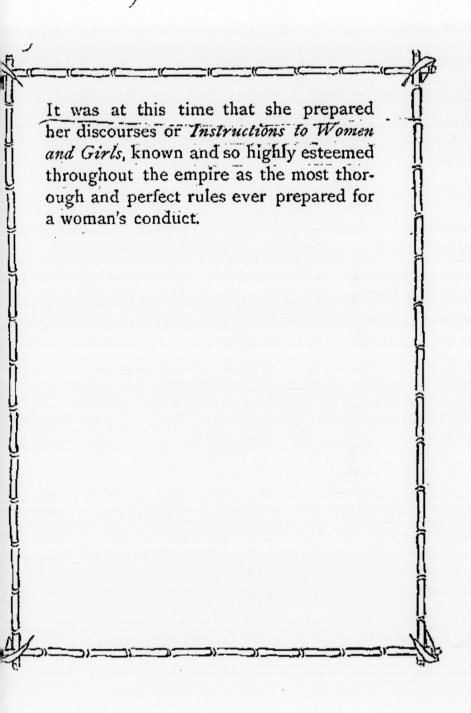

It was at this time that she prepared her discourses or *Instructions to Women and Girls*, known and so highly esteemed throughout the empire as the most thorough and perfect rules ever prepared for a woman's conduct.

INTRODUCTION

TAI KU, your handmaid, is of an illustrious family, and was a philosopher's wife. I have tried to perfect myself in the four womanly virtues, which are: *first*, carefulness in deportment, which includes manners, dress, and all outward conduct; *second*, all womanly duties; *third*, talking little, and that of profit; *fourth*, to be virtuous. Having but few duties, I made books a study. I also earnestly tried to follow the example of the "nine upright women" and "three chaste ones" (ancient Chinese women distinguished for their virtues). It is lamentable that succeeding women have not walked in their footsteps. Because of this I have prepared this book, and desire it to be carefully handed down for the benefit of girls and women.

Chinese Lady Shielding Face with Fan.

CHAPTER I

On the Cultivation of Virtue

All girls, everywhere,
First should learn to cultivate virtue.
Of cultivating virtue's methods,
The most important is
To be pure and upright in morals;
If pure, you are clean inside and outside;
Chastity is your body's glory;
Having it, all your acts shine.
When walking, look straight, turn not
　　your head;
Talking, restrain your voice within your
　　teeth;
Sitting, don't shake your knees—a com-
　　mon fault with men;
Standing, keep quiet your skirts;
When pleased, laugh not aloud;
If angry, still make no noise;
Inner and outer rooms' (women's and
　　men's) duties

Fully understand.

Boys and girls must not together be.

With outside business you have no concern ;

Therefore, go not beyond the court.

If necessary outside to go,

Exhibit not your form,

But screen your face with fan or veil.

To men who are not with you related you may not speak.

With women and girls of not careful conduct you may not associate.

Following virtue, decorum, and uprightness, you so accomplish the end of your being.

Gathering Chia Leaves for Cocoons.

CHAPTER II

Woman's Work.—Weaving Silk, etc.

All girls, everywhere,
Should learn woman's work.
In weaving cloth,
Distinguish between the coarse and fine;
When sitting at the loom work carefully;
When boiling the silk cocoons,
Collecting for them the mulberry and
    chia leaves,
In all be very diligent.
Protect the worms from wind and rain.
If cold, warm them by the fire;
Keep them in a clean place;
As the young ones grow,
Transfer them to baskets, but crowd
    them not;
Provide them leaves, not too many nor
    too few.
Making silk, be careful of the straight and
    cross threads, so you will make a
    perfect piece.

When finished remove the gauze at once
    from the loom.
Cotton cloth fold and lay in boxes or
    baskets.
Silk, cotton, and the two kinds of grass
    cloth,
All learn perfectly to make,
Then you can sell to others,
And yourself have clothing to wear.

Using the Needle

To embroider shoes, stitch stockings,
Mend clothes, and unite cloth,
Trim and quilt garments,
All such work should you be able to do.
If you follow these instructions,
Whether it be cold or warm,
You will have suitable clothing,
And rags and poverty you will not know.
Do not imitate lazy women
Who from youth to womanhood have
    been stupid ;
Not having exerted themselves in wom-
    an's work,

They are prepared for neither cold nor
    warm weather.
Their sewing is so miserable,
People both laugh at and despise them.
The idle girl, going forth to be married,
Injures the reputation of her husband's
    whole family.
Her clothes are ragged and dirty.
She vainly *pulls the west over to cover the
    east*. [*Note:* A sly pull to hide a
    rent.]
She is a disgrace to her village.
I thus exhort and warn the girls,
Let them hear and learn.

Serving Afternoon Tea.

CHAPTER III

On Politeness

All girls, everywhere,
Should learn woman's work.
When women guests are expected,
You should the chairs arrange in order.
Let your own dress be neat and suitable.
Slowly and lightly walk;
Move not your hands about;
And let your voice be gentle and low.
With such deportment
Invite your guests to enter:
Present your salutations,
Inquiring after their welfare since last you
   · met.
In conversation with them,
Talk not at random.
When they questions ask, or answer,
Give most polite attention.
In asking of their welfare,

Or talking of yourself, in a low voice
    speak;
The tea and refreshments carefully pre-
    pare. [*Note:* "Afternoon teas" evi-
    dently are not modern.]
Politely receive guests,
And exhaust courtesy when they depart.
Do not imitate those
Who only regard themselves,
And show no respect to others.
Such receive few guests,
Because they know not politeness.
As a guest, demand nothing;
As a hostess, exhaust hospitality.
When you go to a friend's house
Be not eager to receive attentions.
Having exchanged greetings and taken
    tea,
Immediately your business then make
    known,
This finished, at once rise to go,
Observing all courtesy in departing.
If the hostess prevails upon you to longer
    stay,

And a feast for you prepares,
*Remember the wine to only raise to your
    lips.*
Your chopsticks, place not on the table
    crossed,
But use them with propriety and grace.
The refilling your cup with wine *steadily
    refuse.*
Follow not your desires, just to eat, eat !
Imitate not those rude women
Who with confusion eat, drink, and talk ;
Drinking wine until crazy,
They shamefully vomit their food ;
In this state going home,
Before reaching their house,
Many shameful, rude acts will they do.
    [*Note:* The evils of wine drinking
    were recognized eighteen hundred
    and twenty years ago !]
Outside of your house you should seldom
    go,
Nor into the street for pleasure.
If persons unknown you meet,
Your head and eyes quickly lower.

Do not imitate stupid women
Who gad about from house to house.
These speak many idle words,
And cause others evil to speak of them.
Such may not escape reproof.
Their families by them are injured,
Their parents greatly dishonored.
Still another class imitate not—
Those whose deeds are so evil
That they are shameful, fearful,
And disreputable!

Arranging Dining Room Table.

CHAPTER IV
On Early Rising

All girls, everywhere,
Listen to the following:
Before the sun has fully risen,
At the cock's crowing time
Arise, and dress yourself with care.
Dress neatly, not showily.
Comb your hair and wash your face;
Then at once to the kitchen go;
Of the fire be very careful.
See that the kitchen is clean,
And all the cooking utensils.
Your food *in quantity* and *quality*,
Prepare very carefully,
According to the poverty or riches of
    your family.
In seasoning food,
Observe careful rules.
Be not careless as to whether the food
Shall be sweet, fresh, and fragrant.
Let the cups and plates be clean,

And arranged in order on the table.
Let the three meals be regular,
And properly prepared.
At daylight rising,
Delay not upon the day's work to enter.
Lazy women do not imitate;
They are too idle even to think.
When dark, they go to sleep,
And when the sun is three feet high,
They still are in their beds.
When they rise, it is already late;
But for this they know not shame.
They hasten to the kitchen,
With hair uncombed and face unwashed.
The tea and rice by them prepared
Is scarcely fit to eat,
And all they do is with haste and confusion.
Another class there is you must not imitate.
They think of nothing but eating;
Before the food is fully prepared,
Before their husbands have eaten,
They are eating, here a little, there a little.
Surely this is very disgraceful!
Of such conduct beware.

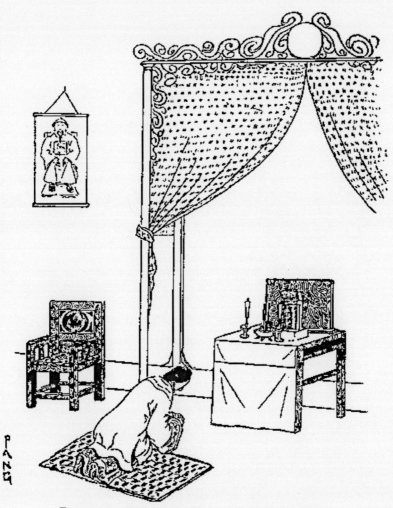

Praying for Sick Parent before Ancestral Tablets.

CHAPTER V

On Reverence for Parents

Girls not yet gone out from their homes
    [not married]
Must carefully reverence their parents;
Early rise, and to them
The morning salutations present.
If cold, build a fire to warm them;
If warm, use the fan to cool them;
If they are hungry, hasten to supply them
    food;
If thirsty, prepare for them the tea.
If your parents rebuke you,
Receive it not impatiently,
But, standing in their presence,
Hear with reverence and obedient heart,
And repent of and forsake the wrong.
The words of your parents,
Regard as beyond all others important;
Obey their instructions;
Turn not away your head,

And be not stiff-necked.
If you do wrong, confess to your parents,
Requesting instruction and reproof.
When your parents become old,
Morning and night be sorrowful and fear-
    ful ;
Their clothes, food, and drink,
With the utmost care provide,
Observing the demands
Of the four seasons in your care for them.
If your parents are sick,
Leave not their bedside,
Loosen not your girdle to lie down ;
The tea and the medicine,
Yourself first taste
To be sure that it is just right.
Cease not to cry unto heaven,
Or to pray in the ancestral temple,
That they may be restored.
Never let it be said
That your parents died
For lack of attention from you.
When they die
Your very bones should grieve,

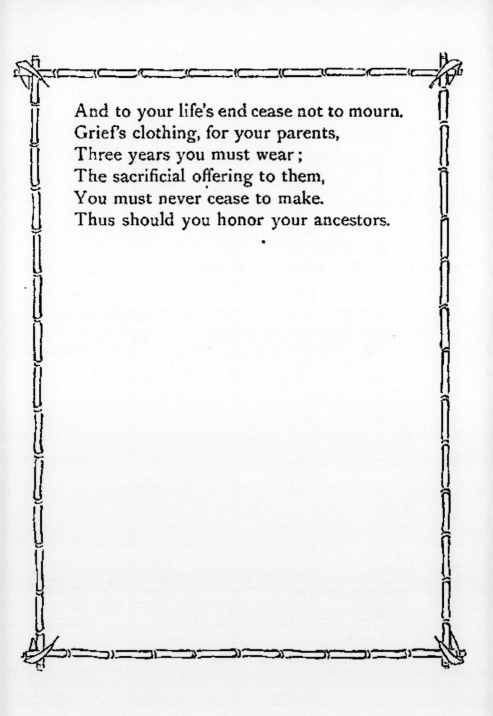

And to your life's end cease not to mourn.
Grief's clothing, for your parents,
Three years you must wear;
The sacrificial offering to them,
You must never cease to make.
Thus should you honor your ancestors.

Making the Bed for Mother-In-law.

CHAPTER VI

On the Reverence Due Father and Mother-in-law

Father and mother-in-law
Are your husband's family.
When you arrive at their threshold
You become a new woman ;
Reverence and serve them
As your own parents.
Honor *greatly* your father-in-law ;
Before him, let neither gladness nor sorrow
Show forth in your face.
Dare not even to *walk* behind him ;
Stand not before him when you speak,
But to one side or behind him,
And hasten his every command to obey.
When your mother-in-law sits
You should respectfully stand ;
Obey quickly her commands.
In the morning early rise
And quietly open the doors,

Making no noise to waken her;
Her toilet articles hasten to prepare;
Her washbowl and towel,
Her toothbrush and powder
All bring together.
[*Note:* Eighteen hundred and twenty
    years ago toothbrushes in China!]
Let not the water be too cold or too hot.
When the mother-in-law wakens,
All these things respectfully present to
    her,
Then immediately retire to one side,
Until her toilet is completed.
Then approach and present the morning
    salutations;
Again retire and prepare her tea.
Quickly and cheerfully carry it to her;
After which the breakfast table arrange;
Place the spoons and chopsticks straight.
The rice cook soft, and
Let the meat be thoroughly done.
From ancient days until now,
Old people have had *sick* teeth;
Therefore, let not the food be so dry

That your mother-in-law
With labor vainly eats.
Daily the three meals
Thus carefully prepare.
When darkness comes,
And your great one [mother-in-law] de-
    sires to sleep,
Carefully for her spread the bed,
When she may peacefully rest,
And you may retire to your room.
Following these instructions,
All your superiors will praise you,
All that know you will esteem you as
    good.
Do not imitate that other class
Who care not for woman's duties.
Loudly they talk before their superiors;
When told to do anything,
They ever answer, " My body is tired,"
When truly they are only lazy.
They obey not their superiors,
Nor care whether they are hungry or
    cold;
The reputation of such is wholly bad;

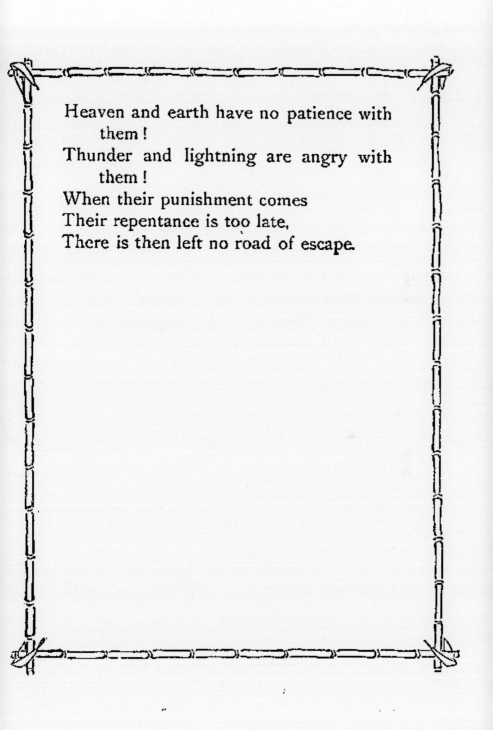

Heaven and earth have no patience with
    them !
Thunder and lightning are angry with
    them !
When their punishment comes
Their repentance is too late,
There is then left no road of escape.

Drinking Wine Together in Marriage Ceremony.

CHAPTER VII

On Reverencing the Husband

When a girl leaves her father's house
Her husband thereafter
Is her nearest relative.
In her former state, before she was born,
Her relations in the present world were
    fixed.
Her husband is to her as heaven!
How dare she fail to reverence him?
The husband commands, the wife obeys;
Yet let there be mutual grace and love;
Let them be *to each other as guests in
    politeness;*
But whenever the husband speaks
Let the wife give careful attention.
If her husband does wrong,
Let her only exhort and persuade him,
And not imitate stupid women
Who call down calamities on bad hus-
    bands.

When the husband goes out
The wife should respectfully ask how far
    he must walk.
If by the middle of the night
He has not returned home,
She may not sleep, but must still wait
    for him,
Keep the light burning and his food hot,
Until she hears his knock at the door.
Do not imitate lazy women
Who go to bed before it is dark.
If the husband is sick,
Let the wife, with careful hand,
Administer all the medicine,
Exhausting every means to restore him,
And failing not to beseech the gods
That his life may be prolonged.
Imitate not stupid women
Who at such times know not sorrow.
If the husband is angry,
Let not the wife be angry in return,
But meekly yield to him,
And *press down* her angry feelings.
Do not imitate bad women

Who are ready to quarrel with their
   husbands.
The winter and summer clothing for the
   husband
Wash carefully and mend neatly.
Let him not be either too cold or too
   hot,
To the injury of his bodily health.
His daily food carefully prepare;
Let not his stomach be empty,
Nor his mouth thirsty,
Lest his body become thin
And his heart sorrowful!
[*Note:* Evidently the charm of a good
   meal for keeping husbands' tempers
   sweet and hearts merry was known
   by our Chinese sisters eighteen hun-
   dred and twenty years ago!]
If your husband is sweet, be you sweet;
If sorrowful, be you sorrowful;
If he is rich, you are rich;
If he is poor, you also are poor.
In life you are one;
In death let the same grave cover you.

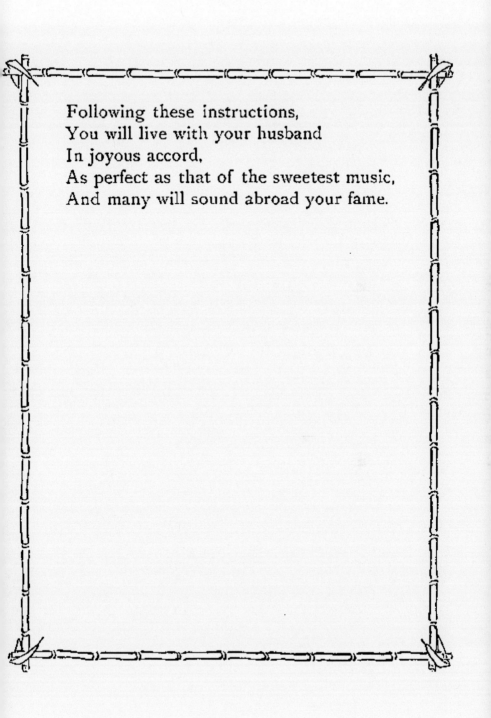

Following these instructions,
You will live with your husband
In joyous accord,
As perfect as that of the sweetest music,
And many will sound abroad your fame.

Garden Scene.

CHAPTER VIII

On the Instruction of Children

Families generally have both boys and
    girls.
When they are three or four years old
It is important to begin their instruction.
This work is truly the mother's.
When old enough to have teachers
The boys and the girls may not study
    together,
But in different rooms, with different
    teachers.
First let them learn politeness;
Afterward their respective duties in life.
Then they may learn to compose
Both poetry and prose.
Their teacher let them obey and rever-
    ence,
And carefully present to him the usual
    gifts.
When first he is invited to teach

Let great politeness be observed,
And no confusion occur.
When the spring flowers open,
And the moon shines at night,
Let the children play in the garden,
And let wine be brought to the teacher;
Ever regard him as one of the family.
The women on meeting the teacher
May only speak one sentence in salutation,
Then immediately retire to the inner
  apartments.
[*Note:* Teachers are treated with the ut-
  most respect, as, being literary men,
  they are of the aristocracy.]
Girls must dwell in the secluded rooms;
Seldom permit them to go outside.
When they are called they must come;
When told to go, let them obey.
If disobedient in the least,
Use small switches and punish them.
The inner rooms' [girls'] instructions
Most carefully observe.
Sweeping the rooms, burning the in-
  cense,

And all the duties of women,
Let the girls thoroughly learn.
Teach them the courtesies to guests,
That they may know how to present
    salutations,
And to restrain their voices;
To carry tea and refreshments to guests,
Walking steadily and with grace.
Let them not be petted and spoiled,
Causing other people to talk about
    them.
Let them not go to other houses,
Lest they cease to respect strangers.
Let them not sing songs,
Lest their voices be heard outside,
And evil words be spoken of them.
Let them not play here, there, and every-
    where,
Lest their deeds become evil.
The present generation's children
Are very bad;
They have learned nothing.
Boys know not how to read;
They grow up following their own wills,

Drinking wine, and seeking only amuse-
ment,
Living idle and useless lives,
Singing songs and dancing,
Disregarding their family duties,
And fearing not their country's laws.
Girls, too, are unwilling to learn;
They are stubborn and talkative;
They know little of woman's duties,
Thus they injure themselves and their
superiors.
When grown, they find themselves dis-
graced.
Then they are displeased with their
parents,
And think not to blame themselves;
Their evil words hurt their parents' ears.
Such girls are worse than wild cats!

Kitchen and Preparing Food.

CHAPTER IX

On Attention to Domestic Duties

Economy and industry
Are the sources of family prosperity;
Industry builds the house;
Idleness will pull it down.
Economy enriches the family;
Extravagance impoverishes it.
Throughout life girls must work.
The whole day's work is in that of the
    early morning;
The whole year's work is in that of the
    spring.
Girls must learn to sweep and clean;
What cannot be swept must be washed.
Think not such work unimportant:
So everyone will see your neatness,
And your whole house will be bright.
In planting the fine grains,
And the cotton seed,
Be not careless and wasteful.

In cooking the rice and soup
Always have the proper heat.
Do not be careless,
And cook this too much and that too
    little,
This too soon and that too late,
So that which might have been good
Is spoiled, and the family's stomachs
Are still empty, and mouths thirsty!
The rice chaff and refuse
Preserve for the animals to eat.
Let them out to feed,
And at the proper time call them in.
Let them not wander away
And trouble the neighbors.
The *husband's money and rice*
Carefully put in a safe place.
Husband's wine and sweetmeats
Do not secretly take!
Let the bins or granaries
Be filled with fine grains.
The soy [a sauce], salt, pepper, and bean
    preserves
Put in properly cleaned vessels.

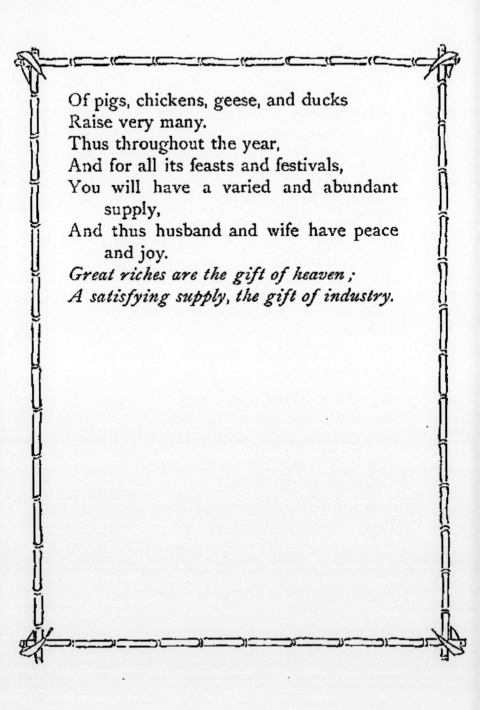

Of pigs, chickens, geese, and ducks
Raise very many.
Thus throughout the year,
And for all its feasts and festivals,
You will have a varied and abundant
supply,
And thus husband and wife have peace
and joy.
Great riches are the gift of heaven;
A satisfying supply, the gift of industry.

Morning Salutation to Male Guest.

CHAPTER X

On the Treatment of Guests

All families should be hospitable.
When a guest is expected
See that the chairs and tables,
Plates and bowls are all in order.
If it is a male guest,
The wife may not be seen,
But, near the reception room,
Await her husband's orders.
If tea is wanted,
See that it is promptly brought.
If the guest remains to eat and sleep,
Wait for the husband to come
And say what he wishes prepared;
Whether to kill chickens and cook vege-
    tables,
Or only offer refreshments.
Carefully see that the seasoning is suitable,
And food properly prepared.
With such care
A wife brings reputation to her house.

If the guest remains overnight,
See that the lamps or candles are in
 order,
His room and bed carefully arranged,
With due reference to the weather,
That the guest may rest in comfort.
With modest face, and low voice,
Present the morning salutations.
In all this you please
Not only your husband, but all his family.
Do not imitate those careless women
Who do not look after the reception room;
Who are hurried and without self-posses-
 sion,
And therefore do nothing properly.
Such are very angry
When the husband invites a guest to stay.
They bring chopsticks, but no spoons;
Salt, but no pepper.
Before the guest has eaten
They are eating;
They whip the boys,
And scold the girls,
And all is confusion.

Such disgrace their husbands,
And mortify the guests.
If a guest arrives
When the husband is absent,
Send a small child to inquire
Whence he comes.
If he looks like a friend,
Send and ask his name
And invite him to enter,
Then with hair in order and dress neat,
The wife may enter the reception room,
And present her salutations.
Then let the tea be served,
And observe all politeness.
After he has taken tea
She should inquire his business,
And if he is a *very* near friend or relation,
She may invite him to await her husband's
    return.
But if he desires to go,
She may accompany him *only*
To the reception room entrance.
I exhort all women
To follow these instructions.

和
順

Neighbors Visiting.

CHAPTER XI

On Gentleness and Harmony

For the family's prosperity,
There are very good rules;
Women should zealously learn them.
Of these, to follow peace
Is of the first importance.
Obedience in all things is the next.
If father or mother-in-law reprove,
Receive it meekly without anger;
If your husband's younger sister or sister-
in-law
Do any wrong, meddle not;
This is not your affair.
Live in peace with both your superiors
and inferiors.
" Whether it is or is not, let it be all the
same to you;
Whether long or short, never mind, do
not quarrel."
[*Note:* A proverb teaching contentment
under all circumstances.]

Tell not the family affairs abroad.

With your neighbors at your right and
left,

Constantly exhaust courtesy.

In visiting with or receiving visits from
them,

In exchanging salutations or congratula-
tions,

Have a *true* heart and pleasant face.

When it is time to talk, talk;

When it is time to do, do!

Let not other people's business enter your
doors.

Imitate not those foolish women

Who have not good principles,

Who are untruthful and unchaste in conversation,

And who dare to be angry with their
superiors.

I exhort all to consider the result of their
words,

Regard the past, and take into account
the future.

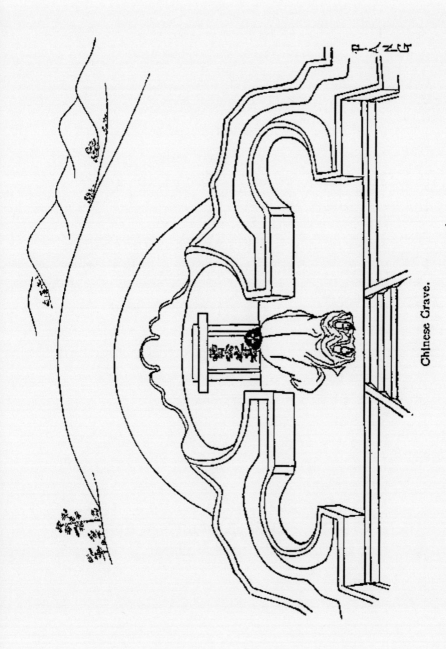

Chinese Grave.

CHAPTER XII

On the Cultivation of Virtue

From ancient times until now
The examples of the "nine upright and
    three pure ones"
Have been ours to look upon.
Their names and characters were recorded
In the national odes, and handed down
    to us.
But how few have followed in their foot-
    steps!
Yet anyone who has the desire and will
May, like them, be good and honorable.
It is of the first importance
To have correct principles;
Next to be pure and upright in act.
If there are male guests in the reception
    room,
Do not go forth from your own room;
If they be even near your own door,
Let not curiosity lead you forth to speak
    to them.

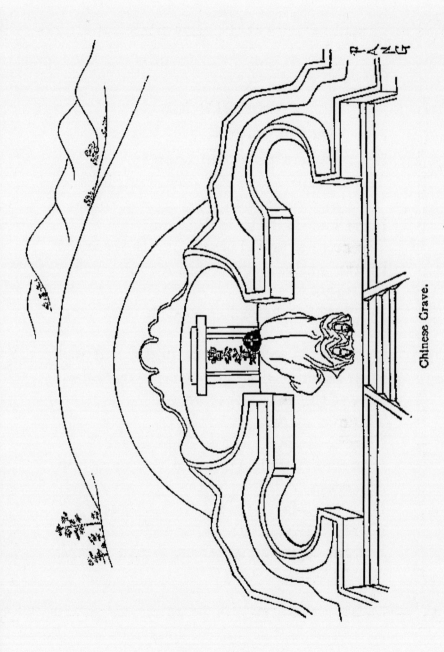

Chinese Grave.

CHAPTER XII

On the Cultivation of Virtue

From ancient times until now
The examples of the "nine upright and
    three pure ones"
Have been ours to look upon.
Their names and characters were recorded
In the national odes, and handed down
    to us.
But how few have followed in their foot-
    steps!
Yet anyone who has the desire and will
May, like them, be good and honorable.
It is of the first importance
To have correct principles;
Next to be pure and upright in act.
If there are male guests in the reception
    room,
Do not go forth from your own room;
If they be even near your own door,
Let not curiosity lead you forth to speak
    to them.

Do not talk secretly with people,
And let not an unchaste thought enter
    your heart.
After the sun goes down, go not from
    your room
To any part of the house without a light.
Lest going into the darkness,
You meet with unspeakable evil.
If you do wrong once,
This may lead to wrong in everything.
One evil act done and a hundred follow.
Heaven determines the relations of hus-
    band and wife ;
This truth is heavier than a mountain.
If you come to misfortune and grief,
If when you have walked but half life's
    road,
Your husband should die,
Then put on the three years' mourning.
Think not of marrying again.
[*Note:* It is very meritorious for a woman
    to remain a widow, and special honors
    are paid her.]
Devote yourself to your husband's family :

Reverence his parents, instruct his chil-
   dren ;
Guard and increase his estate ;
Carefully keep in order his grave,
And observe all the sacrificial rites.
People who are born *must* die ;
This is true of everyone
The heavens beneath.
This book of instructions to women
Is now completed.
If they will but hear and follow,
Their happiness will be immeasurable,
Their light as that of the sun and moon.
Carefully read, remember, and obey.

Printed in the United States
221584BV00001B/69/P